INTO THE CAVE

WHEN MEN GRIEVE

First Edition

by

DR. RONALD G. PETRIE

One to Another Ministries

P.O. Box 1181
Estacada, Oregon 97023
(503) 771-4341

Cover design by **Cornerstone Graphics**

ISBN 1-886153-03-5

Dedication

I dedicate this book to Joyce, Helen, and Vivian, who each taught me in their own way about loss, and love, and hope.

I also dedicate this book to my wife, Joanne, who has supported me and helped me through the most painful time of my life. Most of what I have learned about the process of grief, I have learned from her.

Acknowledgements

I am indebted to Jami Berry, who transcribed my dictation and scrawl, and put it all into book form.

I also want to thank Pastor Bill Griggs who has been a mentor to me and encouraged me to put down on paper what he has observed for many years.

Last, but not least, I want to thank my wonderful neighbors, Pat and Bill Youngberg, who listened to me and were there for me during my deepest grief.

Table of Contents

Table of Contents
Continued

Introduction

Into The Cave: When Men Grieve, is a book that identifies the differences between the way men and women grieve. These differences often lead to misunderstanding on the part of women and children.

The book is written for men, to help them, and in fact, give them permission to grieve. Women will also find it helpful in understanding men that they know who have had a loss.

A man's loss may be from death, divorce, suicide, murder, AIDS, disability, or loss of employment. Any of these calamities can send a man into grief.

If a man embraces his grief and works through it, he will take the path to wellness. If he tries to bury his grief and crawls into his cave, he will be in darkness a long, long time. He has a choice. This book may be the first step in the right direction.

Into the Cave: When Men Grieve

1

. . .

My Story

It was Saturday, March 15th, and we were up at the Grange Hall for a surprise birthday party for Julia, one of our neighbors. There were two to three hundred people there, all eating, drinking, and dancing to the live music.

Joyce and I spent about thirty minutes talking to Rick and Vicki, the couple from whom we had bought our farm. We then split up, each of us talking to different friends and neighbors.

My close friend, Bill, and I were talking when Joyce came up and joined us for a few moments before going to get a drink. I said to Bill, "Doesn't she look great?"

"She just looks radiant," Bill agreed.

I went over to Joyce and said, "Hey babe, how about a dance?"

She laughed and said, "Well, I guess I could take a chance." It was a fast one, and we showed off a little. We had danced together for twenty years and both knew each other's moves. The music stopped and we were both a little winded. She faced me, and I gave her a kiss and said, "I love you."

She said, "I love you, too." I put my arm around her waist, and we started to walk off the dance floor. As we walked, she looked up at me and smiled, and then just fell to the floor dead!

There were paramedics there, and they went to work immediately, but to no avail. She never moved. My life changed forever in that instant.

The next few weeks were a blur. All of my old administrative skills came into play. I took charge and set up all the funeral arrangements. Family and friends came, visited, stayed, and through all of that I didn't cry very much. I was in such a state of shock that I didn't know what I was doing. I was on autopilot.

After two weeks, everyone was gone, and the silence was deafening. I thought I was going to die. I had all kinds of thoughts of suicide. In fact, I perceived that as soon as I had my financial affairs in order that I didn't want to live anymore. I felt that my life was over. I also thought who would want me, why would I want to live, what did I have to offer anyone, and did I even want to have anyone else in my life? At that point, the answer to all of those questions was no, I did not.

About six weeks later, Helen, my adopted mother (she was adopted because I adopted her and her husband as my parents about 30 years before) died. I felt very close to them because my parents had died when I was quite young. Helen and Willie were very close to me. When Willie died, I was asked to perform the eulogy at the memorial service. As time went on, Helen and I met on a regular basis. She asked me to be the executor of Willie's estate, which I gladly did. She also asked me if I would be a partial executor of her estate. Helen was 92 years old, sharp as a tack, and a wonderful feisty woman whom you couldn't help but like. She had great courage and strong convictions. I had lunch with her one day, and about 10 days later I received a call that Helen had died. That did not shock me because at 92 years of age one would expect a person might die at any time. Helen died peacefully. I didn't feel the remorse over Helen as I did over the loss of Joyce, my wife, but still it was another loss in a relatively short period of time.

I sent flowers to the funeral home where Helen's body was taken. They were rejected and sent back. Later, I found out that it was in Helen's will that there was to be nothing. There was to be no memorial service or funeral. She was to be cremated and her ashes destroyed. That made me feel very hollow, like there was something missing. That's when I came to the realization that funerals and memorial services are not for the dead – they are for the living. I still feel like there is an open door that has never quite been closed because I never had an opportunity to say goodbye to Helen and come to some form of closure.

Everyone has a right to indicate how they want their funeral to be or what they want in their funeral, but it certainly was hard on me and her other adopted children not to have any way to show our love and respect for her.

When my wife, Joyce, died, my only sister, Vivian, came out and spent four or five days with me and helped me through that tough time. At that time, she had been diagnosed with cancer. Supposedly, it was the slow-growing type of cancer that was treatable, and she was going to be all right. After I got things squared away with Joyce's funeral, I went back to Arkansas and spent a week with Vivian. We laughed and talked and shared our childhood memories, and had a good time together reminiscing. She was in relatively good health at that time. Approximately four months after Joyce's death, I received another call from my brother-in-law indicating the Vivian was not doing well. I dropped everything and went to Chicago where they had moved to be closer to their children. I spent another week with her. At this visit, she had already become frail and had lost a lot of weight, and it was obvious that she was dying. She had been admitted to the Hospice program and there wasn't much time left for her. I had an opportunity to lie down in the bed next to her and tell her that I loved her, and she told me that she loved me. We were able to say our goodbyes. I left and about a week later she died. I didn't go back for the funeral. It was a private funeral for just her children and her husband.

In a four-month period of time, I had lost the three women in my life who were the closest to me and who I loved. The loneliness that I felt was unbearable. I couldn't stand to be alone. I looked for every excuse that I could to get out of the house. The silence drove me practically mad.

One definition of loneliness is "having love to give and having no one to give it to."[*]

---

[*] *Thanks Joanne*

That certainly expressed how I felt at that time.

From the time of Joyce's death and through the ensuing deaths of Helen and Vivian, I use to sit quietly, privately, in my home and cry. Practically every day I would go over to my neighbor's, Pat and Bill, who always had a cup of coffee and some cookies on the table. I would sit and just talk about what I was feeling and cry, and they would listen. It was the greatest gift that anyone had ever given to me. They didn't try to solve the problem, they didn't try to give me advice, they listened and let me talk. The only thing that they did suggest was that they had heard about grief classes that were being offered by various hospitals, and perhaps it would be helpful for me to attend one. I knew that I needed help because of my background in counseling and psychology. I knew that I was very depressed and suicidal. Taking the grief class probably saved my life.

When I was 15 years old, my father was killed in an automobile accident. My mother and I were taken to a town about 100 miles away to identify the body. He was on a stretcher in the garage of the funeral home with a blanket over him. They pulled back the blanket and his head was almost unrecognizable. It had been caught between the door and frame of the door as the car rolled over on its side. I drove the car back home with his blood on the window to my left, with a partially lit cigarette stuck in the blood. That picture and the one of him lying on the stretcher are imbedded in my mind forever.

When my father died, I don't remember anyone saying anything to me, other than "you have to be strong." I remember not knowing what to say, or what to do, or how to act. I was numb. When I went back to school, the kids and teachers looked at me strangely. No one knew what to say. I remember that it was over a year, before my father's death wasn't in my subconscious and conscious thoughts all the time.

My mother remarried within six months and I didn't get along with my stepfather. I was 14-1/2 years old when I joined the National Guard and just 16 when the Korean War broke out in 1950. The National Guard unit I was in was the first one activated for the conflict. I had just completed my junior year in high school and went with our unit to Colorado for training. The army became my home.

Two years later, I got out of the service, went to college (thank God for the G.I. Bill), and got married. A year later my mother died of cancer.

Of the five deaths that I have experienced in my lifetime, the two that had the most profound effect on me were my father's and my wife's. My father's death changed my life completely. I always thought that I would go into the restaurant business with him and that dream was over. I went into the service and when I got out my mother died and I was on my own. I didn't have anyone to be with or to go to. So I started my own life.

Joyce's death had the same type of profound effect upon me. I didn't know what I was going to do. We had planned our retirement together. She was one week away from retirement, teaching her final class. All the things we planned to do together in our retirement were now gone.

A friend of ours, Carol, related an experience of the reaction of her brother and herself to the death of their father. Carol was with her father on a daily basis and was close to him as she was growing up. She was "daddy's girl." Her brother did not see his father on a regular basis and had lived away from the father for many years. He did not have a strong emotional attachment to his father. Shortly after the father died from cancer after a prolonged illness, the son could not understand why his sister still grieved and couldn't "get over it." He did not have the emotional attachment and couldn't understand hers. He probably never will understand until he has a loss of someone or something that he has a close emotional attachment.

This, and other experiences, has led me to the belief that the closer the relationship you have with a person, the more difficult the loss will be for you. Research has shown that death is twice as devastating when it is unexpected. I'm not sure how you measure twice as much, but I can tell you it is more profound. In looking at my own situation, the loss of Joyce and my father, were the most painful, because I was in a close personal relationship with both of them at the time of their deaths. By contrast, I was not emotionally interdependent with Helen or Vivian or my mother. I did not live with them or interact with them on a regular basis. The closeness of the relationship determines the depth of the pain and grief. That is why two people from the same family may respond to the death of a member of the family in such different ways.

As I indicated previously, about two and one-half months after Joyce died, I was having such a hard time that on the advice of my neighbors I signed up for a grief class at one of the local hospitals.

The class provided a safe haven for me as a man to let out my grief. The people in the class were all like me, having suffered major losses through either death of divorce. Those emotions had been bottled up since the time of my wife's death. The process and the content of the class gave me insights and understandings of what I was going through and ways to cope with the changes that were going on in my life. When I took the class, the general content and process were very helpful and as I indicated had probably saved my life, but one of the things that struck me was there seemed to be some very profound differences between the way men and women grieve. As a result of that experience, I started reading what was available (that wasn't much) about men in grief. Some of the experiences I was having didn't seem to go along with what I had read.

2

. . .

Pain, Confusion, and Loneliness

When Joyce died that night, literally in my arms, I sat on the bench against the wall while the paramedics worked on her. I knew she was dead. I heard that last breath escape her lips, and I begged God to bring her back. After thirty minutes they told me she was gone. I went to her now cold body, closed her eyes, and kissed her for the last time.

I was numb. A young couple who had both lost their mates and had married each other, sat down next to me to console me. They offered to come and stay with me that night. I thanked them but said no. Two of my neighbors also offered to come stay with me, but I said no. I wanted to be alone. I wanted to cry by myself. I crawled into my cave. I didn't sleep that night or the next. My mind was reeling with the "what ifs," "should haves," and "did I miss some sign?"

As I already stated, all my old administrative skills that I had let go came back into focus. Phone calls to make to friends and family, death notices, planning the funeral, the cemetery plot, the memorial service later, a million details. The friends and relatives came. There was the hubbub of activity.

"How are you doing, Ron?"

"I'm fine," or "As good as can be expected." These were my answers.

At that time I didn't cry very much and was in such a state of shock that I was not functioning other than to take care of basic things. It was at that time that most people thought that I was doing well. I wasn't showing very much emotion, and the response from most people was "He's really handling it well." The opposite is actually the truth.

Most people think you are doing well if you are not crying or showing outward emotion. When you are crying and you are showing emotion, that is, in fact, when you are walking through the grieving process and you are learning to cope again with the realities of the world around you. When we show the most pain is when we are making the most progress.

We need to grieve. Grief is not something to be ashamed of, but rather it is what we need to do to become whole again.

After two weeks, everyone was gone. Back home, back to work, life as usual. Except for me. In four months, the three women who were closest to me were gone. The loneliness I felt overwhelmed me. The silence was deafening. I had never experienced physical pain around my heart before, the heaviness, the constriction, the ache. I had heard of people having a broken heart. I always thought that it was a figure of speech. It's not!

I slipped into depression. As soon as I had my will and financial affairs in order, I planned to take my life. Thank God it took many months before that was all settled.

For five months I did not eat one meal at home. Not breakfast, lunch, or dinner. At night I sat watching T.V. and would realize that I had been watching something for thirty or forty minutes and didn't have a clue what I had been watching. Nights and weekends were the worst.

I was so depressed I couldn't do anything. I had no ambition, no motivation, no drive. My sleeping was sporadic and unrestful.

One of the most important things that I learned in life was that although you may not have control of the circumstances of your life, you have complete control over how you react to those circumstances. It was a message I gave repeatedly to Upward Bound students that I was responsible for, and other students that I advised and counseled. It had worked for me many times in the past as I was confronted with life's obstacles and disappointments.

This time it was different. I needed someone to blame, someone to be angry at, someone to fight. God!

A well meaning, but misguided, person said to me, "It's God's will that Joyce died. It's part of his plan for your life."

That made me livid, and at that point I hated God for taking Joyce away from me.

It has taken me some time to resolve that issue and realize that God doesn't make sickness and disease. When Adam and Eve were in the Garden of Eden and chose to sin, our world was no longer a perfect place. Disease, sickness, and tragedy became part of that imperfect world. God helps you to pick up the shattered pieces of your life, put them back together, and go on. He helps you find new directions and purposes, if you'll let Him!

I met Joanne when I took the grief class about 2-1/2 months after Joyce and Helen had died. Joanne is the Hospice Chaplain for one of the local hospitals and had been developing and teaching the grief class for fifteen years, since her late husband, Duane, died. After the class was over, we started to date and five months after Joyce's death, we were married.

I was still in very deep grief at the time of our marriage, and I continued to work through the grieving process. Joanne has been there for me and has continued to love me and be supportive of me. Many women would be jealous and threatened by my love for Joyce. Joanne is not. In fact, she thanks me for sharing Joyce with her and has come to love Joyce, too.

We have the capacity to love more than one person. Joanne has shown me that. I love Joanne for her compassion and for her love that she gives to me, and for her understanding. She knows that I love her even though I grieve over the loss of the love that I had for Joyce.

I have had many loves in my life. I loved my mother and father. I loved my sister. I loved my adopted mother. I loved Joyce. I loved my former wife. I love my children. I've loved some very special dogs and cats in my life. And I've loved a number of different people in various degrees.

Bob, a friend of mine, related a story to me about a friend of his who had been divorced six times. The man was an outstanding athlete, good looking, and financially well off. The women that he married were all very attractive, but after a year or two (and the honeymoon was over) they all left him for someone else. It sounded strange. Then Bob told me that this fellow gives monetary things to his wives, but did not know how to give of himself. He does not know how to love someone. All of his life, everyone gave to him, but somehow he never learned how to give the most important thing – love – in return.

As human beings, it is a natural part of our makeup to love, to share, to give of ourselves and to receive love in return. That is what makes us human beings. That's what makes life worth living. Everything else in life is just "stuff." Nothing else matters if we don't have someone to share life.

This reminds of the quote from C.S. Lewis, "To love at all is to be vulnerable. Love anything and your heart will certainly be wrung and possibly be broken. If you're to make sure of keeping it intact you must give your heart to no one. Not even an animal. Wrap it up carefully around with hobbies and little luxuries. Avoid all entanglements. Lock it up safe in the casket or coffin of your selfishness. But in that casket safe, dark, motionless, airless, it will change. It will not be broken, it will become unbreakable, impenetrable, irredeemable— the only place outside of heaven where you can be perfectly safe from all the dangers of love-is hell."

~ MY FRIEND GEORGE ~

The loss of an animal can be just as traumatic as losing a human being. Many animals become very close to us by giving their complete love, devotion, and loyalty to us. They don't care (or notice) if we're short, tall, fat, thin, ugly, or beautiful. I think animals (particularly dogs) look at you and see your soul. They accept you without qualification.

One of the first dogs that I become one with was a German Shorthair Pointer named George. I'm a pheasant and duck hunter, and have field trailed* for many years. George, to this day, was the best bird

* Field trials are competitive events whereby dogs are judged against a standard for there ability to find game (such as pheasants) point the bird, hold while the bird is flushed, and retrieving the bird to hand after it has been shot. Usually the handlers are on horseback.

dog I have ever seen, and I've seen the best in the country.

Larry, a graduate student of mine who had an extensive background in Field and Show dogs before I became involved in those endeavors, went hunting with me several times and told me, "Ron, you may hunt and field trial the rest of your life and never again find a dog as good as George." It's been thirty years since George was killed by an automobile, and I never have.

George was my buddy. Wherever I was, he was by my side, lying at my feet. Whenever I went somewhere, George would go with me and lay on the passenger side on the floor of the car. He lived to hunt, and he lived for me. When he was killed, I didn't go to work for three days because of my grief. His hand-painted picture adorns my living room wall. Even today, thirty years later, tears come to my eyes when I think of him.

Is it all right to have those kinds of feelings for a dog, cat or horse? Of course!

We all need to love something or someone and be loved in return. Our hearts are big enough to love more than once, with a variety of persons and pets.

If you're fortunate, you have experienced the unconditional love of another person or persons. If you've had one or more George's in your life, you know what I'm talking about when I say unconditional love! Maybe God put animals in our lives to remind us on a day-to-day basis of his unconditional love for us?

3

What Men Need

~ GRIEF CLASS ~

A number of times when I have talked with people about the need to take a grief class, I have made the statement that the class has content and a process. The two of them together produce a gestalt (which means that the end product is more than the sum of the parts). You will not "get over" the loss of someone by burying it or ignoring it. The only way that you become well and healed is to embrace your grief, to realize that it is a process that you are going through, and that you need to go through that process in order to finally become healed again.

Unfortunately, most men refuse to take that approach but rather try to forget the person that they have lost. They do this by not talking about the person or trying to do anything that would remind them of the person. I must admit that when I first lost Joyce, I wasn't sure what it was that I was suppose to do because it was painful. Everything that I did that reminded me of her was difficult, from getting rid of her clothes to taking down pictures. I did that very quickly, much quicker than I really should have. Somehow I had the mistaken notion at that time that that is what I needed to do in order to "move on."

When we are going through grief, we have a number of needs. One of them, which I have alluded to before, is to have someone listen, to have someone to be there for you. Another area that we need desperately is to have people around us. I used every excuse that I could during the "deadly silence" to be around people. It is imperative that people that you love be around you. One of the greatest gifts that my youngest son gave to me was that he called me at least once or twice a week. We had lunch or coffee or played golf or did something at least once a week. He was just there for me. What a gift!

The third thing that we need a great deal of is personal touching. One of the things that you miss so much is the hugs, the kisses, the touching, and the proximity of the other person whom you loved. It is very difficult to all of a sudden be deprived of physical touch. It's part of what makes us human and part of what we need to sustain our humanity.

It's easy to die. It takes great courage to go on and rebuild a life after someone you loved has died and left you.

~ CULTURAL AVOIDANCE ~

Generally speaking, we have a cultural avoidance of death and dying and grief in our society. We don't talk about it as part of any normal experience; we avoid it at all costs. We don't deal with it unless it is thrust upon us. One of the other things that I observed is that between men and women, women usually have an easier time with the grieving process because they have a support system.   This support system consists of other women, friends, and family who share their feelings and grief. Women are allowed, and in fact encouraged, to share their emotions openly within our society. Men are not.

Men usually have no such support system of friends and family to talk with about their personal, emotional feelings. Men are perceived as, and in fact are, independent and autonomous. To share grief with someone is a threat to that autonomy.

If a man reveals himself to another man, he risks being vulnerable. We are raised to be strong. We are raised not to cry. We are raised to be the leaders in times of adversity. When men talk with one another, they tend to talk about sports, fishing, or whatever, but they don't talk about personal emotional things. Unless they have gone through some very traumatic experiences themselves, they don't know how to listen or to act. When I was going through my toughest times, I had several men friends that I tried to talk to. After about five minutes I could tell that they were so uncomfortable with the topic, and with trying to deal with it, that they looked for an excuse to either get out or get away or to change the subject. When two men are talking, and one of them brings up a problem, the other man basically looks for some way to solve the problem. He's interested in what can be done about solving the problem, not the emotional connections that are related to the problem.

Men are usually interested in taking action. They want to see that something is <u>done</u>.

~ MEN DON'T CRY ~

For a man to show grief is an admission that he couldn't handle it. That is hard for most men to do under the best of circumstances. I can remember when I was a little boy (I must have been around seven or eight years old), and I had fallen down and skinned my knee and I came into the house crying. My father proceeded to put some Mercurochrome on the scratched knee as I was crying profusely. I'll never forget what he said to me. "Quit your crying or I'll give you something to cry about." I had to quit crying or I would be in deep trouble with my father. Men are supposed to be strong and tough.

Recently, I was watching the "Biography" television program on A&E about the life of Ethel Kennedy. It was chronicling the terrible burdens that the Kennedy's, and her in particular, went through. She lost two children and her husband. Interestingly, if you remember the deaths of JFK and Bobby Kennedy and the whole Kennedy clan, you didn't see anyone in their family crying outwardly. A comment was made in the Biography program that "Kennedy's don't cry." In the case of the Kennedy clan, the burden of suppressing their grief, at least in a public way, was shared by the women as well as by the men. In most cases, it's the men that are expected to carry that burden alone.

Grief is a burden and men don't want to lay that burden on anyone else. It's theirs to have and it's theirs to bear.

~ INTO THE CAVE ~

Most men have a very difficult time grieving openly. Consequently, they withdraw into their cave and tend to grieve privately. I can't tell you how many times I sat alone, by myself, and cried and cried and cried. That's not necessarily bad. In fact, it's good because it releases the stress and the strain of the grief and allows it to leave your body.

~ MEN AS LEADERS ~

Men in a group put off talking to one another until they know that they have the respect of other men in the group. They'll wait it out and see the lay of the land before they move on. In a family situation, it is usually the man that's responsible for being the leader in times of crisis. A case in point, (you may remember), was the death of Bill Cosby's son, Ennis, who was killed in a random act of robbery and murder while he was changing a tire on the freeway. A lady in one of our classes said to me that Bill Cosby must not have loved his son very much because when he read the statement to the press, he seemed unemotional and didn't cry and was matter of fact. I asked her whether she saw Mrs. Cosby anyplace and she said no. Bill Cosby, as the head of the family, was responsible for keeping it all together.

There is an exception to the scenario of the man being responsible for the leadership of the family, and that is where there is a mother raising children on her own and there's no man around. That may have been the case with Ethel Kennedy. In that situation, it frequently falls upon the woman to assume the role of the man, as well as the women, and suppress the outward emotions for the perceived sake of the children.

4

. . .

Taking Action

When men grieve, they want to take action. They want to do something to show their respect for the loss they have had. They will establish a scholarship, write a book, plant a tree, put together a photo album, or any number of things that are action-oriented. They want to do something. I didn't know that until I looked back at my own actions. After Joyce died, one of the first things that I did was establish a scholarship fund in her name with the educational media association that she had been the president, and had been very active. It was a very normal thing for me to do to show my respect for her. If you came to our home, you would see an island out in the front of the driveway. There is a pink dogwood tree in that island. That is the "Joyce" tree. If you looked out our kitchen window, there is another dogwood—that is the "Duane" tree. This one was planted in the memory Joanne's late husband.

Another case in point is Bill Cosby. His son, Ennis, had some type of learning disability. I'm not sure of the exact problem or condition, but Bill Cosby established the Ennis Cosby Foundation as a memorial to his son. That would be very typical of what a man might do.

There are exceptions to the rule, of course, but generally speaking, most men have trouble expressing themselves verbally, especially as it relates to emotional problems related to grief. Men want to take some form of action; by contrast, women want interaction.

Women frequently misunderstand man's private and quiet grief. Many times it is mistaken for indifference. It's not.

~ GRIEF SUBSTITUTES ~

Men may use aggression, anger, violence, or drinking as grief substitutes. They may act out in ways that apparently have nothing to do with the grief that they are going through.

When a man relates his grief to others, particularly to another man, it can be very powerful in helping the healing process. The interesting thing about men is that they will usually open up to a woman, because women are not seen as a threat to their masculinity. A woman who sees a man cry or show emotions may perceive him as being sensitive and caring. That is acceptable to the woman as well as to the man.

There are some other statistics about men in grief that says a lot about what happens to them. Fifty percent of all widowed men remarry between three and six months after the loss of their spouse. They remarry because they are so terribly lonely. Remember what the definition of loneliness is - "having love to give and no one to give it to." [*]

Another interesting statistic is that men over 65 years of age that do not remarry within two years usually die. Obviously, there are exceptions to this, but the statistics support it. What do they die from? Loneliness. They give up.

_____

[*] *Thanks Joanne*

5

Death of a Child

Nine out of ten couples have severe marriage problems after a death of child. Three out of four divorce within two years, and only one couple out of five remains married five years after their child dies. These terrible statistics are in part because of the different ways men and women grieve.

If the couple had been having any sort of marital problems before the death of the child, the problems become compounded with the death of the child. When a woman loses her child, her grief is deeper and different than the relationship that the man has with the child. The woman has born that child; it has come from her womb. She has a different relationship with that child than the man does. This does not mean that the man does not love the child. It doesn't mean that he doesn't feel compassion, but at the time of loss, the man is expected to be strong. In fact, he may have a difficult time expressing his emotions to his wife, and he tends to withdraw. The wife then thinks that he doesn't care, and the husband thinks she is overreacting. They start to lose respect for each other.

~ BIOLOGY AND EMOTIONS ~

After some time, weeks, months, the man has the biological need for intimacy. In fact, he may need intimacy to relieve the stress of the loss. The woman's need for intimacy is bound up in emotions. The man's is first of all bound up in biology and then emotions. The man separates his biological needs from the loss of the child. The woman cannot. Intimacy is emotional for women first and biologically secondary. It is the opposite for men. Pretty soon, after some period of time, the man and wife are in separate bedrooms, there is no longer any communication, and divorce becomes the option.

In any grief situation where couples are involved they tend to go through the grief on different schedules and with different expressions of emotion. At the time that a couple is going through grief as a result of the loss of a child, they both are in such terrible pain that they really have very little to give to each other. Each one expects the other one to take care of the pain and to help to ease the problem. Neither one is capable of doing it at that time.

~ LOSS THROUGH MISCARRIAGE ~

When a couple loses a child through a miscarriage in the early or late stages particularly, there's a very different response from both the husband and the wife. I recently observed this in a young couple that we knew when there was a miscarriage in the beginning of the second trimester. The husband did not respond to it at all other than to indicate that it was a sad thing. He had a difficult time understanding why his wife was emotionally distraught over the loss of the fetus. To him it was just that, a fetus. It had no human life, it had no personality, it was not a person. The mother, by comparison, had really strong feelings about it, and in fact, went through a grieving process with the loss of the child through the miscarriage. She was the only one that knew or had a feeling for that child that never made it into this world.

Recently, I heard about a young couple who lost a child very late in the pregnancy. The wife was emotionally distraught. She had carried the child for almost nine months. She heard its heartbeat and felt it move and kick. She experienced its life and was emotionally attached to it. The husband did not have that same type of attachment. He could only imagine what his wife felt. When the baby did not survive, the wife went into deep grief. At first, the husband was not very supportive. Her grief was beyond his comprehension emotionally. He was able, however, to realize that his wife needed support and that he needed to help her through the grieving process.

They secured a gravestone and have continued to go through the ritual of saying goodbye to a relationship that never had a chance to fully develop.

The husband was a wise man for realizing that his wife needed him for support at this very difficult time.

6

. . .

Saying Goodbye to the Living

There are a number of different kinds of losses that are not final. Such is the case in divorce, a broken relationship perhaps, relocation, empty-nest syndrome, serious changes in our health or that of someone we love, or a family member who has Alzheimer's disease.

These kinds of losses pose different problems in the healing process. The person or persons that we have loved no longer love us or are out of the picture as is the case in divorce or Alzheimer's, and yet they are still with us because of children, (in the case of divorce), or because the person is still alive, (as in the case of Alzheimer's). We deal with these different emotions in different ways. We must learn to say goodbye to the relationship as it existed and can never exist again but it is not final. We have a more difficult time coming to closure when the relationship is not final.

In dealing with divorce, many people suffer from anger, hurt, loneliness, hopelessness, abandonment, rejection, and failure. Another word related to divorce is humiliation.

There are 1,000,000 divorces in America every year. According to recent statistics, 65% of all marriages will end in divorce. If you do not take the time to work through the pain of divorce and remarry within two years, the divorce rate is an astonishing 83%.

Much of the reaction in a divorce depends on whether you are the divorcer or the divorcee. That is, are you the person who initiated the divorce or you are the recipient of the divorce. In the case where you have divorced the spouse, you may feel vindicated or feel that you did the right thing because of circumstances that you could no longer tolerate. If you are the divorced person, you may or may not have those kinds of feelings, and in fact, may very well feel like a victim. This happens in many cases where women are deserted by their husbands for another woman, or for reasons that do not make sense to the women. The unfortunate part of no fault divorce is that is takes two people to get married and it only takes one person to get divorced. If both parties are not willing to go to counseling to try to work out their differences and to bring about the changes that are necessary to save their marriage then it is pretty well doomed.

~ FORGIVING AND LETTING GO ~

One of the first steps of working through divorce (assuming that it's inevitable and everything has been done to try to save it with no success) is to learn to live through the adversity and the humiliation of the divorce and learn how to say goodbye to the pain and to forgive the other party. Forgiving our self is another important step in the process. This obviously is not easy. We cannot change what has happened, but learning to let go and release the pain helps us to have the courage and the faith to grow and to change. One way to accomplish this is by rituals.

~ RITUALS ~

Rituals are symbolic meanings that can be learned and played out through an action to represent who you are or what you believe to be important. Rituals help us deal with the transition of pain and help us let go.

Writing can become a very beneficial ritual. You may write a letter to your former spouse in which you acknowledge his or her qualities and thanking them for the good memories that you have and indicate that you hope that you can still be friends and treat each other civilly. You might also write down all the things that you are going to say goodbye to. Such as her nagging, her drinking, her bad temper, her foul-mouth, etc., and then also to make a list of what you're looking forward to in the future...

❖ A positive happy relationship with someone else.

❖   Lack of depression as a result of dealing with her bad temper.

❖   A positive attitude about the rest of your life.

After Joyce died, Joanne and I went to the beach one day, and for some reason I was feeling quite angry. I snapped at Joanne and was not very nice. She said to me, "What's the matter, Ron? What's bothering you?" I replied that I wasn't sure, but the more I thought about it, the more I came to realize that I was angry because Joyce and I planned to come to the beach and we never made it. And here I was with Joanne and I was taking it out on her without realizing what I was doing. Joanne suggested that I perform a ritual to say goodbye to that which I was no longer able to do.

We went into town and bought a Mylar balloon and had it filled up with helium. We came back to the beach, and I openly stated out loud that I wanted to let my resentment and my anger go and ask for God's help in going through this difficult time. I released the balloon and watched it fly away and felt a heavy burden being released from my shoulders.

~ JOURNALING ~

One of the things that Joanne taught us in grief class was that journaling could be a very effective ritual to relieve our pain. I personally don't care to journal on a day-to-day basis, although it is very helpful for a lot of people. What I did do, though, (at one point), was to sit down and write over fifty pages of my feelings. I wrote for five or six hours until I had writer's cramps so bad that I had to quit. This was great catharsis for me because I was able to release the pent-up feelings that I had. This was one way to do it.

~ GUILT ~

When we suffer the loss of someone close, we may experience guilt associated with "what if's," "should have's," and "why didn't I's." Joanne tells of the situation about her daughter, Amy, and her late husband, Duane.

Duane had offered to take Amy to the Portland Trail Blazer games on several occasions. Amy (who was 18 years old at the time) was always busy with other things and passed up the opportunity to go with her dad to the games.

The night before Duane died of a heart attack, Duane offered to take Amy to a game and she said she had something else to do. The next morning Duane was dead, and Amy was overcome with grief and guilt. "Why didn't I go?" Woulda, coulda, shoulda! She couldn't forgive herself for not going with her dad. She carried that burden for some time. One day Joanne suggested to

Amy that what she might do is write a letter to her dad telling him how she felt. Amy worked on the letter for a week. She poured her heart out. The letter was very long. After she had written it, Joanne sat down with her and had her read the letter out loud. When she finished (after much crying), Joanne said, "Now, I want you to write a letter from your dad to you; writing what you think he would say in reply to your letter."

This letter was much shorter. Basically it said, "I love you and forgive you." She knew her dad. This ritual relieved the great burden of guilt that had been so heavy on her heart.

~ TALKING ~

Talk, talk, talk, talk, talk, talk. Talking helped me a great deal. Get it out! Find a good listener. Someone who will not try to solve your problem-just listen. You may have to teach them how to listen to you. The more I was able to talk through my grief and what I was feeling, the sooner I was able to move on in my life. The more I suppressed my feelings, the longer it took me to get on the road to recovery.

One of the things that can happen to you if you don't learn to release your anger is that you may become very bitter. Bitterness is like drinking poison and waiting for the other person to die. * The person that it kills is you. We have to learn to forgive and to put aside our anger and bitterness over the loss that we've had. If we don't, it will eat us up.

~ SKIN HUNGER ~

One of the biggest problems that we face when we have lost someone through death or divorce is that we miss the kisses

---

* *Thanks Richard Green*

and the hugs and the intimacy that we had with that person. In the case of divorce, (particularly if we were the person that was divorced), we have a tremendous need to prove that we are still attractive to the opposite sex. This is a time when both men and women have a tendency to become promiscuous. We need to prove to ourselves, and to everyone else, that we are still a desirable person. The unfortunate part of fulfilling that need for touching and loving is that in our despair and loneliness, we may mistake loneliness for true love, only to find out in a short period of time that we may not have been in love at all, but that we were in love with love. The person that you have transferred this love to may not have any of the characteristics or qualities that you really need for a long term, sustained relationship. That is why there is an 83% divorce rate for second marriages when the people have not fully gone through the grieving process before looking for another mate.

7

. . .

Developing a Support System

As I indicating in an earlier chapter, women tend to have support systems consisting of friends and family with whom they share their emotions. But men, by and large, do not have such support systems. As my wife, Joanne, has stated to me a number of times, women talk face to face, and men talk side by side. That is, women talk to each other, men talk about things with each other, but, do not talk directly to one another about emotionally and personal things.

If we want to get well and get through the healing process and the grieving process, it is necessary for us to embrace our grief. We need to move forward with it, we need to express ourselves. We will not grow and develop if we try to bury our feelings.

If we bury our grief and refuse to look at it or take it head on, we will continue to make mistakes in new relationships and never completely recover from our loss.

The first step towards healing is to admit that we need help. This, again, is difficult for many men to do. Asking for help is a sign of weakness. It reminds me of stories about men who refuse to ask for directions when driving because somehow it's an indication that they're not in control of the situation.

Working through grief is some of the hardest work you will ever do. The grieving process itself is not meant to be a solitary journey. Many people never fully release grief because they refuse the help of their friends and family.

What we are looking for in a support system is loving, caring people who are willing and available to help us. They should be willing to help us physically, emotionally, and spiritually. Some men sabotage their support systems by whining, self-pity, or manipulation. Be honest, be vulnerable, and be willing to take responsibility for yourself so that people will want to help you.

Vulnerability means being willing to express personal needs, admitting your own limitations or failures, having a teachable spirit, being reluctant to appear the expert, the answer person, or the final voice of authority. I would also add to not be ashamed to let your emotions show.

Most of us have not had the experience of going through grief, and therefore, don't know how to go about it or where to go for help. If you feel uncomfortable with some members of your family because you have always been the leader and the strong one, there are some other alternatives to consider. If you have a church, call your pastor and ask him or her about where you can get help. You might be able to get help directly from the pastor. Most local hospitals have Hospice programs that have support groups for people who have had a loss of their mates. There may also be local groups available through colleges, United Way, or other civic organizations. Check them out. The most important thing is to go someplace for help. Asking for help is not a weakness. You will be no less of a man for doing so.

If you are looking for a friend to be a listener (either man or woman), be sure to look for someone who is patient, discreet and available. Don't depend on only one person to help you through the difficult time. You'll wear out one person. Find several that will be available on a round-the-clock basis. You may need to teach the person how to listen.

The following guidelines may help:

- When I ask you to listen to me, and you start giving advice, you have not done what I asked.

- When I ask you to listen to me, and you begin to tell me why I shouldn't feel that way, you are tampering with my feelings.

- When I ask you to listen to me and you feel you have to solve my problems, you have failed me, strange as that may seem.

- So, please, just listen and hear me, and if you want to talk, wait a few minutes for your turn, and I promise I'll listen to you.

If you have a friend who asks you if you need help, say "yes." Don't withdraw from caring people. Be responsive to people from different age brackets. Maybe you can find people from work, from church, from your neighborhood, or from your family. Don't be afraid to sit down and tell your support people what it is that you need.

One of the biggest problems that I had when I was in deep grief is that I had a terrible time going through the mail and paying the bills. The first time Joanne came over to my house, she couldn't believe my kitchen table. I had mail stacked up two and three feet high all over the table. I just couldn't bring myself to go through all that mail. She sat down and sorted out those things that I needed to take of, such as the bills and important papers, and then helped me throw away the junk mail that I was not able to sort through before.

Another thing I was not able to do during my time of heaviest grieving, was to clean the house. I think that is probably typical of most men, we are not use to doing that on a regular basis. So, through the help of some friends, I found a cleaning lady to come in and help straighten the place up. It made me feel better when she had finished cleaning the house. It reminded me of how it use to be and perked me up.

At first a lot of people brought over food, which was very much appreciated. After a short period of time, however, I seemed to be getting a lot of the same dishes. When some of the ladies would ask me what it was that I really liked or disliked, I told them. Don't be afraid to share your feelings on things like this. I like tuna fish, but I don't like it every day.

After some time (a few weeks), people will start to withdraw their support of "things." That is, bringing over food or stopping by to say hello. Their life is going on, and their time is limited. Don't think that they're letting you down and that they don't care about you. It's hard for anyone else to walk in your shoes at that time. And remember, they all have their lives to lead, too.

As I have indicated before in this book, taking a grief class through a local hospital or Hospice program is one of the best things that I ever did. There was a group of people who were experiencing the same types of problems that I was experiencing, and who knew where I was coming from. These people helped me to express my feelings in a safe, private environment. I could let it all out without feeling embarrassment.

~ BIG DECISIONS ~

One of the things that you'll be told by a lot of people when you're going through grief is to not make any big decisions. This is especially true of financial decisions. If you have financial decisions to make, seek out a professional financial consultant who has been personally recommended and checked out by someone you trust. You need that help. You may not be thinking as clearly as you think you are.

~ INANIMATE SUPPORT ~

If you are having difficulty talking and relating to someone on a personal basis, but you're looking for help, there are a number of good sources available. One of the first ones that I would recommend, of course, is the Bible. However, if you're not feeling that you need spiritual help at this time, there are a lot of good books available in the library. Go talk with your librarian and look up what might be available, such as books on grief. Another book that I would recommend is the book written by Joanne and myself entitled "How to Say Goodbye; Working Through Personal Grief." It is a much more detailed account of the process than I am attempting in this book.

One of the things that I have found that really was helpful to me was to visit the grave of my late wife, Joyce, and talk to her and tell her how I felt. Maybe you have a photograph at home that you could look at and talk to, if you don't want to go visit the gravesite. It helps to release your feelings; to get them out where you can hear them. This allows your emotions and the stress to escape your physical body.

~ MUSIC, MUSIC, MUSIC ~

There is a lot to be said for listening to music that can help you to process grief.

Classical music seemed to be the most helpful in terms of soothing me and making me feel more calm and relaxed. Popular songs that may have been special to you and your loved one, (though they make you cry and be sad and lonely), can also help you to remember the good things and the good times that you never will or should forget. It may take a long time before you're able to listen to some of the special songs without tears coming to your eyes. When you can listen to them and you don't break down, you know that you are on the path to healing and recovery.

~ TIME TO LAUGH ~

When we're going through deep grief, we don't feel very much like laughing. In fact, we may feel that it's an insult to the one we have lost to laugh about anything. We can only stay down and depressed for so long. At some point, we need to see the "normal" side of life again. A good laugh has somewhat of the same effect as a good cry—it releases our stress and tension. I frequently look to "Peanuts" in the newspaper for a good laugh. Some people like the "Three Stooges" or "Bob Newhart" or "Tim Conway." Experience whatever gives you joy and laughter. It's O.K.! You had a sense of humor before and you still do. It's just been inactive for a while. It's another step down the path to recovery.

~ REACHING OUT ~

When we are going through grief, we are intently focused on ourselves, and our loss. All I could think about for weeks and months was Joyce's death and what it was doing to me. Looking back on it, I do not think that my preoccupation with that event was abnormal. I cannot say that I remember the exact time or situation that made me aware that I was starting to get better, but I do remember that I began to help Joanne teach the grief classes by teaching a session on "Men in Grief." I started to try to help someone else who was hurting and it made me feel better. Helping someone else (be it a child that needs your comfort and reassurance, or have a cup of coffee with someone else who has had a loss and listen to them, or a neighbor that you help build a fence) helps to get you on the track again and do something positive. "Reach out and touch someone" is a slogan that is very good advice. It will help you to heal.

Into the Cave: When Men Grieve

8

. . .

Special Days

The holidays are a particularly difficult time for a lot of people going through grief. Because of the death or divorce of a loved one, things are not the same. Family gatherings are different. You miss that special someone you shared these times with in the past. Birthdays and anniversaries are also times when you may be flooded with grief because you miss the person so much.

I awoke the morning of March 15th, and lay in bed thinking about what had happened on this date four years before. This was the day that Joyce dropped dead in my arms on a dance floor.

A wave of grief hit me and tears came welling up in my eyes. The last few days I had been anxious in anticipation of this day, as I have been for the past three years. It's been four years now, and although things are better, I still have my days and still have my moments.

Yesterday as I was driving in my car, I had some Willie Nelson CD's playing, and it seemed that every song reminded me of her. I loved her so much.

When I awoke that morning after lying in bed for a few minutes, I got up and went to the kitchen to get a cup of coffee. There on the island in the kitchen, a candle was burning. There next to it was a note and a card. Along with these were a bunch of fresh daffodils that Joanne had cut and put in a vase. The note said,

> "Dear Ron,
>   Flowers planted with love
> willingly given to honor Joyce's
> life and her grave. Please place
> these on her grave today.
>   Joanne"

I opened the Hallmark card. It was red with a gold tic-tac-toe drawing on the front. The tic-tac-toe had hearts diagonally placed from one corner to another with a line drawn through them. Inside the card, it read, "Cross my heart, I love you." Joanne wrote inside, "Dearest Ron, whatever you do today, you will be in my thoughts and prayers. I am so thankful God brought us together so we could share the past, present, and future as best friends. With love and kisses, Joanne."

On the opposite page, a note said, "On March 15th, four years ago, your life changed forever. You and Joyce started your day just like every other day, but before the day was over, your heart was broken and stabbing with pain. Today as you recall the events of losing Joyce, I want you to know that I admire your courage to take the journey through grief. I love you for loving Joyce and sharing her with me. I love you because you make room in your life for me."

I went to the cemetery with the bouquet of daffodils that Joanne had left for me. I set them on Joyce's grave, and talked to her one more time. We had twenty years together, and there are many memories of wonderful times. I now know that it's all right to remember. Other dates and days that are special are Joyce's birthday and our anniversary.

I think the important thing to remember is that it is not disrespectful to Joanne for me to have memories and grief of my life with Joyce. Just as there is no reason for me to be upset or jealous of

Joanne's twenty five years of marriage and remembrances of her late husband, Duanne.

Many people feel that it is wrong to have memories of someone that you've lost and to talk about that person. That's nonsense. You had a life with them and that cannot and should not be erased.

There is a poem by Terry Kettering that says is very well...

The Elephant In The Room

There's an elephant in the room.
It is large and squatting, so it is hard
*   to get around it.*
Yet we squeeze by with "How are
*   you?" and "I'm fine."...*
And a thousand other forms of trivial
*   chatter.*
We talk about the weather.
We talk about work.
We talk about everything else –
*   except the elephant in the room.*
There's an elephant in the room.
We all know it is there.
We are thinking about the elephant
*   as we talk together.*
It is constantly on our minds.
For, you see, it is a very big elephant.

It has hurt us all.
But we do not talk about the
*   elephant in the room.*
Oh, please, say her name.
Oh, please, say "Barbara" again.
Oh, please, let's talk about the
*   elephant in the room.*
For if we talk about her death,
Perhaps we can talk about her
*   life.*
Can I say "Barbara" to you and
*   not have you look away?*
For if I cannot, then you are
*   leaving me*
Alone . . . in a room . . .
With an elephant.

I want to qualify the previous remarks. If you make a shrine out of the person and put them on a pedestal, and if you talk about them all the time, you've missed the point. You need to put their passing in perspective and learn how to say goodbye to that relationship, as it no longer exists. As I've indicated before in a previous chapter, we have the capacity to love more than one person in our life. I loved Joyce, and I love Joanne. They are not mutually exclusive. I do not have to give up my love for Joyce to love Joanne.

~ CEREMONY OF REMEMBRANCE ~

At Christmas time each year, Joanne has a ceremony of remembrance, in which all of the people who have taken grief classes or who have been involved with her support groups, come together for a night to honor their departed family. Joanne's "One To Another" Ministry secures some very special ornaments that are made in the form of a heart. A nametag is secured to the heart identifying the person that is no longer with us. In the ceremony, the families come up to the tree and place their ornaments on the tree and say the person's name out loud. The first year that I attended the ceremony of remembrance, I bought an ornament for Joyce, Helen, and Vivian. After the ceremony, the ornaments were taken off and placed on our Christmas tree at home. I also bought additional ornaments and gave them to my children so that they would have them to put on their own trees to remember our loved ones at this very special time. This is a special ritual that can help you make it through Christmas holidays in a more positive way.

Embrace your grief—don't deny it. Don't bury it. Don't crawl into your cave. Seek the path that will lead you to being whole again.

9

. . .

New Normal

As you go through the grieving process, at some point you will come to feel that you are ready to go on with your life, to give it new meaning. This is what Joanne and I call "new normal." You're not the same as you were before; you're a new person ready for a normalized relationship. Joanne and I teach dating classes for people who are ready to go on with their lives. One of the most important things that we do in the dating class is to have the participants sit down and make a list of the qualities that they are looking for in a mate. The qualities go well beyond the height, weight, and color of the hair and eyes, etc., which many people start with. It starts with looking at the things that are really important in a relationship. These characteristics might include things like:

- ❖ Religious preferences
- ❖ Commitment to God
- ❖ Even-temperedness
- ❖ Good sense of humor
- ❖ Willing sexual partner
- ❖ Animal or pet person
- ❖ Athletic or outdoor activities

After the class members have completed the task of identifying the qualities they are looking for in a mate, we have them do the more difficult and more important task of identifying what they have to give to someone else. Are you a good provider? Are you kind and loving? Are you compassionate and understanding? Do you have a good sense of humor? Are you willing to give and take? What is your religious commitment?

When we started dating, Joanne had such a list, which she shared with me. She knew what she was looking for in a mate and what she had to give in return. I made a similar list and shared it with her. These lists, and discussions which followed, gave us both insight and understanding of each other. I believe it helped to build our marriage on a solid foundation.

~ LOOKING FOR A NEW MATE ~

After you have gone through the process of making the list of the qualities that you want in a mate and making a list of qualities you have to give to a relationship, you now have the task of reaching out and doing something as you start to look for someone else to share your life.

There is a good possibility that someone who would be a good candidate for you could be close around you. You may have friends or family who know of someone who might be appropriate for you. Don't be afraid to go out on a blind date.

Remember it's a numbers game. You might have to go out with five or ten or a hundred people to find the right person for you. Although that may sound discouraging, it's very unlikely that you'll meet the perfect person the first time out.

You'll probably scratching your head and saying, "Well, where do I start to look to find a decent person to spend the rest of my life with?" Singles clubs, dating services, singles organizations through your church, and "Introduction" ads in the newspapers are all places to start.

When I first started looking actively for someone, one of the first things I did was place an ad in the local "Introduction" section of the newspaper. This may sound crass upon the surface, but it isn't necessarily a bad way to start. I put my ad in the paper and lo and behold I received 27 responses in the first day. I was amazed and overwhelmed. I screened through the 27 responses and selected 6 that I felt might be appropriate matches. I went out to coffee, lunch, and dinner with the different ladies and found them all to be nice. They were all looking for the same thing I was looking for, and were taking the chance of revealing themselves. Unfortunately, none of the six ladies that I went out with ended up being a good match. I liked some of them, some of them liked me, but there was no real spark that told me "this is the one."

There was one lady that I dated four or five times, thinking that she might be suitable, only to find out over time that she raised some red flags in me. She was dishonest about several things and I found that she appeared to be quite possessive and jealous by nature. For an example, she got very upset when I called her "Joyce" by accident instead of her own name. She made a big deal about it. Those sorts of things can and do happen when you first start to date, it's normal and it's natural. You called your mate by that name for a long time and it's a habit.

When you start to date someone and you're serious about them, pay attention to warning signs of possible problems—the so called "red flags." For instance, if your adult children see the person as unacceptable, listen to what they have to say and why they feel that way. They may not be right because they are comparing that person to the person you've lost through death or divorce. No one could possibly measure up. But if their concerns are about the person's character or honesty, etc., weigh them carefully.

Don't play games! Be yourself and treat the other person the way you want them to treat you.

Love, companionship, and the relationship that you have with another person is God's greatest gift. It is worth pursuing. There is a passage in the Bible about love. It states,

> "Love never gives up.
> Love cares more for others than for self.
> Love doesn't want what it doesn't have.
> Love doesn't strut,
> Doesn't have a swelled head,
> Doesn't force itself on others,
> Isn't always "me first,"
> Doesn't fly off the handle,
> Doesn't keep score of the sins of others,
> Doesn't revel when others grovel,
> Takes pleasure in the flowering truth,
> Puts up with anything,
> Trusts God always,
> Always looks for the best,
> Never looks back,
> But keeps going to the end."

I Corinthians 13:4-7
The Message

These are powerful truths. To live by them in your relationship with your spouse will surely lead to a happy and positive relationship.

God speed!

Joanne and Ron Petrie are available to speak to your church or organization, or to offer seminars and speaking engagements related to grief. Contact them at:

One to Another Ministries
P.O. Box 1181
Estacada, OR 97023
Phone: 503-771-4341